TUDOR
1485–1603

STUART
1603–1714

GEORGIAN
1714–1837

D0188038

70001481425 4

Haringey Libraries	
NN	
Askews & Holts	07-Dec-2011
942.1	
	HAOL23/8/11(2)

Children's
HISTORY of
LONDON

Written by
Jim Pipe

HOMETOWN WORLD

How well do you know your city?

Have you ever wondered what it would have been like living in London when the Plague struck? What about going to see the Great Exhibition in 1851? This book will uncover the important and exciting things that happened in this wonderful city.

Want to hear the other good bits? Some rather brainy folk have worked on this book to make sure it's fun and informative. So what are you waiting for? Peel back the pages and be amazed at London's very own story.

THE FACTS

Timeline shows which period (dates and people) each spread is talking about

Intriguing photos

Fun Facts to amaze you!

'Spot this!' game with hints on something to find in the city

THE EVIDENCE

Go back in time to read what it was like for children growing up in London.

Each period in the book ends with a summary explaining how we know about the past.

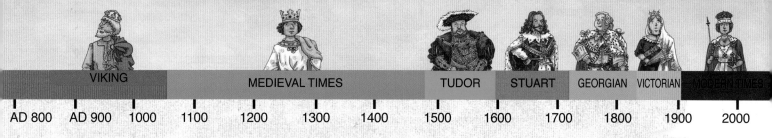

Contents

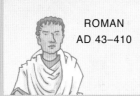
Islands in the Marsh

In a small fortress built above a marshy swamp, dark-haired locals crowd around a tall blacksmith as he shows off his sword. It's made from iron, much tougher than the bronze weapons they own. The stranger is a Celt, one of a group of newcomers from Europe. Fearless in battle, they are also skilled craftworkers. It's 200 BC and already London is a great place to do business!

Roundhouse walls were made from woven branches covered in mud mixed with animal poo!

You wouldn't find me collecting dung for the roundhouse walls. I'm a warrior!

Early Settlers

The first settlers in the area that is now London arrived over half a million years ago. They lived alongside herds of mammoths, horses and giant deer. Around 12,000 years ago, modern humans like us began to settle down in the valley alongside the River Thames, which is still important to London today. When the Celts arrived in Britain, early Londoners were already trading slaves, corn and metal goods with merchants from Europe.

3500 BC EARLY LONDONERS GROW THEIR OWN CROPS...200 BC FIRST COINS APPEAR...

A Holy River

In ancient times, the centre of London was a great marsh. At high tide it became a lake, turning nearby hills into islands. In fact, the swampy ground south of the river remained a marsh for many centuries. To the ancient people living nearby, the Thames was a holy river. They threw precious items like weapons, mirrors, brooches and cauldrons into the water as gifts for spirits, gods and goddesses.

SPOT THIS!

Statues of London's two guardian giants are part of the Lord Mayor's Show.

FUN FACT

The letters 'ea' or 'ey' were often used on the end of a place name to mean 'island', as in Chelsea, Battersea and Bermondsey.

Celts are known for making pottery, colourful jewellery and fabrics.

London Legends

There are many legends about ancient London. One says the city was founded by Brutus, a prince from the ancient city of Troy. When Brutus came to Britain, he supposedly beat two giants, Gog and Magog, in a wrestling match. The Trojan prince then chained them to the gates of his palace. It's said the pair have guarded London ever since!

How do we know?

Most of what we know about ancient London comes from objects that archaeologists have dug up. Fragments of pots and bowls and stone and metal tools have been found all over the city, many close to the twin hills of Cornhill and Ludgate Hill. We also know a lot about early Londoners from the piles of rubbish they left everywhere! The remains of ancient settlements have also been discovered, such as Yeoveney Lodge near the modern town of Staines. Some London street names come from Celtic words, such as Maiden Lane and Ingal Road.

5

The Romans are Here!

Sylvia is excited to be exploring her new home in Londinium. The mosaic floors in this villa are even more beautiful than the ones in their villa in Rome. Sylvia's father looks out at the rain and tuts loudly. It's a good job there is underfloor heating to keep them warm in this horrible weather!

This yew tree in St Andrew's churchyard in Totteridge sprouted around 2,000 years ago!

Roman coins show the ruling emperor. This helps historians to work out dates.

London is Born

Almost 2,000 years ago, Julius Caesar led the first Roman invasion of Britain. Though he reached the Thames Valley and defeated a large army led by the local chieftain Cassivellaunus, Caesar didn't stay long.

A hundred years later, in AD 43, the Romans returned, this time for good. Within a few years they had built a fortified town beside the Thames. They called it Londinium – the future London. The old British settlements nearby were already a centre for trade. Soon London was a prosperous town with up to 100,000 people living there.

Hundreds of foreign craftworkers came to London to make a living. From bakers and wine dealers to potters and jewellery makers, there was money to be made in all kinds of trades. Londoners were eager to get their hands on fine Roman goods.

... 55–54 BC JULIUS CAESAR INVADES BRITAIN... AD 50 LONDINIUM IS FOUNDED...

Burned by Boudica

Not everyone was happy about Roman rule. In AD 60, the Iceni tribe based in East Anglia revolted after the Romans forced some of them to become slaves. Their queen, Boudica, crushed a Roman army sent to capture her, then headed for London. Her soldiers burned the town to the ground, killing everyone in it.

Though the Roman governor eventually defeated Boudica, the town was in ruins. Amazingly, within 30 years, the Romans had rebuilt most of London.

A giant statue of Boudica in her chariot stands near to the Houses of Parliament.

FUN FACT
A bright red layer of soil about 4 metres below today's streets marks the destruction of London by Boudica.

The New Capital

For the next 300 years, London was by far the largest city in Britain, and its capital. London became a centre of government and law as well as trade, allowing the Romans to run the whole of Britain from one city. London grew around the wooden bridge across the Thames. From here, half a dozen roads led to the rest of the country.

People from all corners of the Roman Empire made London their home. I'm from Greece!

SPOT THIS!
The London Stone lies behind an iron grill in Cannon Street. It may be a Roman milestone.

...AD 60 BOUDICA DESTROYS LONDON...AD 60–90 THE CITY IS REBUILT...

7

Building London

Roman London was built in a neat grid of streets on a low hill north of the Thames. The town also spilled over onto two islands on the far side of the bridge. A high wall protected the main town from enemy tribes.

The heart of Londinium was a busy market square surrounded by temples, shops and government offices. Major buildings included a giant hall, or basilica, where the town council met, an amphitheatre for entertainment (now buried below the Guildhall) and several public baths.

A typical Roman fort →

A large fort near today's Barbican housed up to 1,000 soldiers!

A Bustling Port

Down by the Thames was a long wall, or quay, made from massive oak beams. This was filled with warehouses, large bundles of goods, and men busy loading and unloading ships.

Goods came from all over the Roman Empire: glass and bronze from France, marble from Greece, and pottery jars filled with olive oil, fish sauce and wine from Italy and Spain. These items were loaded onto carts or smaller boats for delivery to the rest of the country. In return, London merchants traded slaves, hunting dogs, oysters and lead. The Roman roads leading out of London made it easier to transport goods and this helped the port grow and develop.

Roman ships like the one in this model carried goods to Britain from all over the Roman Empire.

...AD 120 FIRE IS STARTED ACCIDENTALLY AND QUICKLY SPREADS THROUGH LONDON...

At the Temple

There were temples throughout the city. Roman Londoners worshipped Celtic and Eastern gods as well as Roman gods such as Jupiter. They made sacrifices in return for favours or advice. They also nailed up trinkets or small statues at local shrines. Some of these offerings have been found along the banks of Walbrook stream which ran through the centre of Roman London. When they died, Roman Londoners were buried or burned in cemeteries along the main roads leading out of the city.

SPOT THIS!

Remains of the Roman walls can be seen near Tower Hill underground station.

Like us, most Londoners live in dark, damp houses made from mud bricks or woven twigs and clay.

FUN FACT
The original Roman walls around the City of London were 6 metres high. If you were on patrol duty, you couldn't be scared of heights!

Home Time

Most Londoners were crammed into small family dwellings or cheap rented rooms in the centre of town. These were usually small single-storey buildings divided by narrow alleys. Cooking, washing and sleeping were all done in the same room. A small yard at the back was used for keeping animals or dumping rubbish.

Wealthy Londoners lived in spacious townhouses or in fine villas outside the city walls. Built of stone, they had glass windows, painted walls, beautiful mosaic floors and underfloor heating. A few villas even had their own private bathhouse.

The Romans finally left Londinium around AD 410, to defend their crumbling empire from invaders. Within a generation, the Roman way of life had almost disappeared.

Roman Londoners enjoyed feasts, board games and music at home. They also went to the amphitheatre, where they watched boxing matches, executions and wild animals fighting.

Here a young Roman slave boy, Martial, describes a trip to the baths. This was where people relaxed and caught up on gossip as well as washing off the city's grime.

I like nothing more than watching a good execution at the amphitheatre!

My master, Gaius Silvius Tetricus, is a rich merchant. He is always in a foul mood until he's had his daily trip to the baths. While he's taking it easy, I run errands.

Once at the baths, my master spends most of his time chatting in the steam room. Afterwards I help to scrape him clean using a strigil - a curved blade made of bronze. Then he takes a quick plunge in a cold pool.

The bit I hate most is helping my master to put on his toga. It's very hard to make the long robe hang in the right way. If I get it wrong I can expect trouble.

My master is very proud to be a Roman citizen. He looks down on Londoners who wear woollen leggings or tunics, even though they're much better suited to the chilly weather here!

Jars like this one were used to store wine, fish sauce and olive oil.

Dogs like me left pawprints in clay tiles made by Roman tilemakers.

Clever doggy!

In the basement of an office block in Thames Street lie the remains of a complete Roman bathhouse!

How do we know?

All sorts of objects have survived from Roman London, including tombstones, cooking knives, charred food, storage jars, bronze helmets, sandals, glass flasks and even leather underwear that may have been worn by an acrobat!

In 1962, a Roman shipwreck was discovered in the Thames, dating from around AD 150. We also have a good idea where the Roman bridge was from all the coins dropped by travellers into the riverbed below, not far from where London Bridge is today.

In 2002 and 2003, a large Roman bathhouse was excavated at Shadwell in east London. Remains of baths were also discovered at Huggin Hill in Upper Thames Street.

By studying the skeletons of buried Romans, archaeologists can work out where they came from, what they ate and how healthy they were. For example, many had terrible problems with their teeth!

CELT 500 BC	ROMAN AD 43–410	ANGLO-SAXON AD 450–1066	VIKING AD 865–1066	MEDIEVAL TIMES 1066–1485

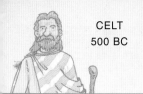
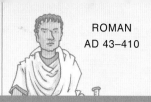

New Invaders

It is a long time since the first Saxons arrived here. The story of their voyage and arrival on the muddy beach has become a favourite tale, told around the fire at night. But now everyone is panicking. There's a rumour that new invaders have landed and are going to attack the city with a great army. It's the Vikings! Some people flee into the countryside while others prepare to defend London Bridge.

FUN FACT

Originally, Westminster Abbey sat on Thorney Island, created by two branches of the river Tyburn as it flowed into the Thames.

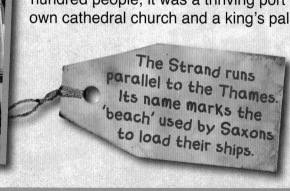

London Reborn

By the 6th century AD, London was a ruin. Invaders from Germany – the Angles and Saxons – had conquered most of southern Britain. They were farmers, not city folk, and lived in villages along the Thames. Roman London was all but abandoned.

In the early 7th century, however, a group of Christian monks breathed life back into the old city. Within 100 years, a new trading town that the Anglo-Saxons called Lundenwic had sprung up near to where Covent Garden is today. Home to several hundred people, it was a thriving port with its own cathedral church and a king's palace.

The Strand runs parallel to the Thames. Its name marks the 'beach' used by Saxons to load their ships.

Viking Raiders

London's new wealth made it a tempting target for Viking raiders from Denmark and Sweden, who sailed up the Thames in their dragon-headed longships. Though Londoners beat off several attacks, a huge Viking army took over the city in AD 871. Fifteen years later, the Saxons fought back under King Alfred the Great and recaptured the city. To protect themselves against further Viking raids, they built a new settlement – then called Lundenburgh – inside the old Roman walls.

English	Origin
Monday	Moon's day
Tuesday	Tiw's day
Wednesday	Woden's day
Thursday	Thor's day
Friday	Freya's day
Saturday	Saturn's day
Sunday	Sun's day

Our days of the week come from the Saxons except for Saturday, which is Roman.

Kings and queens of England have been crowned at Westminster Abbey for over 1,000 years.

Royal Power

In the 10th century, London once again prospered, despite suffering two large fires and a terrible plague. By the 11th century, it was the wealthiest and largest town in Britain. Winchester had been used as the Saxon capital but London now took over as capital once again.

The Anglo-Saxon King Edward the Confessor built a palace at Westminster, so he could oversee the building of his new abbey. Although Edward's original palace has gone, Westminster Palace has remained the centre of government ever since.

SPOT THIS!

This plaque near Southwark Bridge remembers King Alfred.

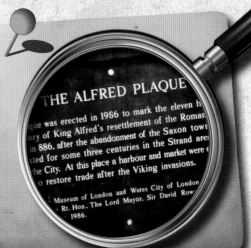

THE ALFRED PLAQUE

...que was erected in 1986 to mark the eleven h... ...ary of King Alfred's resettlement of the Roman... ...n 886, after the abandonment of the Saxon town... ...sted for some three centuries in the Strand are... ...he City. At this place a harbour and market were ... ...o restore trade after the Viking invasions.

Museum of London and Wates City of London... ...Rt. Hon., The Lord Mayor, Sir David Row... ...1986.

CELT
500 BC

ROMAN
AD 43–410

ANGLO-
SAXON
AD 450–
1066

VIKING
AD 865–
1066

MEDIEVAL
TIMES
1066–1485

The great events of Saxon times were reported in chronicles. Written by monks from the time of Alfred the Great onwards, they recorded all the important events that had happened each year, such as battles, plagues or the death of a king or queen.

Here's how a chronicle might have described what happened in AD 994, when a Danish army led by King Sweyn Forkbeard tried to capture London.

The Anglo-Saxon Chronicle is a record of key events in Saxon and Viking times.

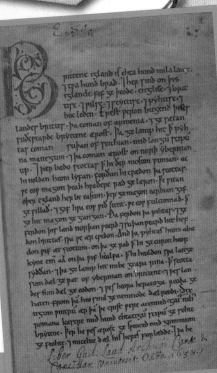

King Sweyn went east at the head of a great army, hoping the people of London would bow down to him. But they resisted and forced the Danes back.

Again the Vikings attacked, this time taking hold of London's bridge. To the rescue came the Norwegian prince Olaf Haroldson, a friend of the Saxon king Aethelred. The Danes showered Olaf's men with spears and arrows. But they protected themselves by pulling the roofs off nearby houses and holding them over their heads.

Getting close to the bridge, Olaf's soldiers tied ropes to it then rowed downstream as hard as they could. Helped by the strong tide, they made the bridge collapse.

Sweyn lost many men in the battle and was forced to give up the attack.

14

Viking panpipes!

These Viking shoes once had smelly Viking feet inside them.

How do we know?

Much of what we know about Anglo-Saxon and Viking Londoners comes from the objects they buried with their dead, such as swords, brooches and jewellery. A grave slab belonging to a Danish noble was found near St Paul's Cathedral around 150 years ago. The cathedral church and king's palace of Lundenwic no longer exist, so how do we know they were there? The church appears on the Bayeux Tapestry and remains were later found beneath the new Westminster Abbey.

London was made up of lots of small villages at this time.

St Magnus the Martyr church, near London Bridge, is dedicated to a peace-loving 11th-century Viking.

A Growing City

A young girl sneaks past the guards collecting a toll at the southern end of London's famous bridge. They're busy gawping at the heads of rebels stuck on poles above the drawbridge. Below, merchants move goods up and down the river. The main street across the bridge is narrow, crowded and dark. A heavy cart rumbles past and the girl darts out of its way just in time.

Norman Invasion

When Edward The Confessor died in 1066, he left no heirs. The battle to succeed him was won by his cousin, William the Conquerer, ruler of the Normans. William defeated Harold, the Anglo-Saxon leader, at the Battle of Hastings.

After London surrendered, William built a castle in the southeast corner of the city. This is the White Tower at the heart of the Tower of London. William also granted the city a charter, allowing Londoners to keep their ancient laws and freedoms in return for paying taxes.

Hold onto your heads, traitors!

Fresh Talent

After the Norman invasion there was a flood of new arrivals in London from northern France, including many Jews who set up businesses in the capital. Many worked as moneylenders and helped to finance the growing city. The arrival of Flemish and French cloth workers also gave a huge boost to London.

Let's Build!

The Normans were great builders. They turned London into a real capital city, building the Great Hall at Westminster, the Guildhall (London's town hall) and the first stone London Bridge. Though a great fire devastated London in 1087, the Normans soon rebuilt the city. Their magnificent new cathedral, St Paul's, dominated London's skyline for another 600 years.

The Tower of London was a royal mint, a treasury and also a zoo in medieval times.

FUN FACT
The first stone London Bridge was finished in 1209. It survived over 600 years until a new bridge was opened by William IV in 1831.

SPOT THIS!
Prince Henry's Room at 17 Fleet Street dates back to the 12th century. Can you spot it?

I am called William the Conqueror because I conquered all of England.

Rich and Powerful

During the 1190s, Henry Fitz-Ailwin became London's first mayor. To win over the wealthy merchants of London, King Richard I allowed the city to govern itself.

By the mid-13th century, London was one of the largest cities in Europe, with a population of 80,000 people. It was richer than the next nine biggest towns in England put together.

London was home to the first Parliament in the 13th century, as well as the law courts and the Exchequer, which organized the royal finances. The city was also an important religious centre. It had 100 churches within its walls – more than any other city in Europe.

Living in the City

Medieval London had to grow in size to keep up with the booming population. It grew in a very unplanned way. Within the city walls, the houses of ordinary Londoners had thatched roofs with clay and timber walls. As London grew more crowded, the houses grew taller and the cobbled streets narrower and darker. The top floors hung over the street, perfect for flinging waste out onto the street below! When fires broke out, they quickly spread to nearby houses.

Rich merchants, barons and churchmen bought large, fine houses built of stone, often with courtyards and gardens. Many of these were along the Strand, the road linking the main city to the king's palace at Westminster.

Ewww – rotten eggs! Being a medieval criminal really stinks!

People enjoyed throwing rotten food at criminals locked in the local pillory.

One of London's few remaining medieval churches is St Bartholomew the Great, West Smithfield.

Filthy

For all its magnificent buildings, the capital was filthy. By medieval times, London was an open sewer. Toilets called garderobes emptied straight into the streets or the Thames. Soot, dust and mud covered everything in grime. The smell of dung mingled with the stink from the tanneries and the fish markets. The streets were dark, crowded and chaotic, with market stalls running up the middle. London was also very violent. Gangs beat up passers-by and riots were common. Londoners were banned from going out after 9 pm in summer.

TUDOR 1485–1603 | **STUART** 1603–1714 | **GEORGIAN** 1714–1837 | **VICTORIAN** 1837–1901 | **MODERN TIMES** 1901–NOW

Black Death

With the dirt came deadly diseases like the Black Death, which killed half of all Londoners in just 18 months. Even in plague-free years, poor Londoners were lucky to live to 30. There was little help for people who couldn't find work, so there were many beggars. Even those with a job were often badly fed and lived in shacks. Hundreds of Londoners died from starvation every year, especially in years when the harvest failed.

FUN FACT One medieval fashion was to wear 'poulaines' – long, leather shoes with pointed toes stuffed with moss to make them stiff!

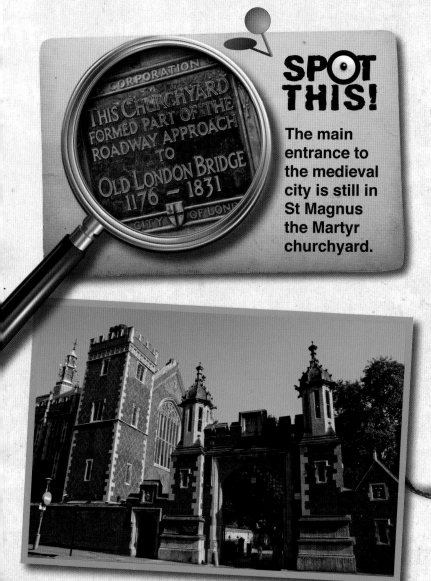

SPOT THIS!

The main entrance to the medieval city is still in St Magnus the Martyr churchyard.

Tough Times

As well as famine and plague, London was hit by a long war with France in the 14th century. The city's troubles continued with the Peasants' Revolt in 1381, when thousands of peasants stormed the Tower of London, protesting against a new tax. After the revolt fizzled out, the heads of its leaders were put on spikes and displayed on London Bridge as a warning to other rebels.

By around 1550, business was booming again. London's busy port was the centre of the European wine and wool trade. Different groups of craft workers, such as goldsmiths, butchers and weavers, formed clubs known as guilds.

The Inns of Court are home to London's lawyers. The Old Hall dates back to 1489 and the Gatehouse was built in 1518–21.

Known as the 'Great Plague' in medieval times, the Black Death spread more quickly in big cities, partly because many large families lived in a single room. The rats that carried the infectious fleas feasted on the city's rubbish, which was often thrown out of windows.

Here, a young boy called Walter describes the horrors of the plague.

Buboes are ugly black swellings caused by the plague.

People in medieval times didn't know about germs or disease. They invented very strange cures!

The whole city lives in fear of this grievous disease. It kills horribly, and spreads with frightening speed. No one, noble or peasant, is safe.

The pox starts with a black swelling the size of an egg in your armpits and groin. Soon your body is covered in boils and black blotches. Some who catch it at night are dead the next morning!

Every day, the morning light reveals new piles of bodies, dragged out of homes and left in front of doorways. No doctor or medicine can stop this plague. So many corpses are brought to the churches each hour they must be buried in huge trenches by the hundreds.

For some reason, I have been blessed. I caught the disease and survived, though the buboes remain on my arms and legs.

How to Cure the Plague

Step 1: Find a live frog.

Step 2: Put the frog's belly on the plague sore.

Step 3: Wait for the frog to swell up and burst.

Step 4: Repeat with further frogs until they stop bursting.

Wormwood, comfrey and vinegar – that should cure you!

London was so disgusting that city councillors passed this law in 1349.

To the Lord Mayor of London: Order to cause the human dung and filth lying in the streets to be removed. The city is so foul with the filth from out of the houses that the air is infected and the city poisoned.

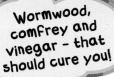

How do we know?

Westminster Abbey, the White Tower and Temple Church are among the dozen or so medieval buildings still standing in London. Other remains include a mass burial of plague victims uncovered in Spitalfields and stones from the old London bridge. Smaller objects have also been discovered, from leather shoes and wax seals to arrowheads and pieces of woven cloth.

All sorts of interesting documents survive from medieval times, including church, town, military and guild records. The Royal Charter of King John in 1215 confirmed that Londoners could choose their own Mayor. Handwritten books and manuscripts containing poems, stories and chronicles also survive. When William Caxton set up the first printing press at Westminster in 1476, it allowed books to be printed cheaply in large numbers.

In the 1400s, Lord Mayor Dick Whittington paid for a giant public toilet that could seat 100 people!

What's in a Name?

Some of the district and street names in London have remained the same for 1,000 years or more. Others have disappeared as buildings were torn down or new streets were built. Old place names can provide helpful clues about who lived in a particular area, what buildings were once there, and even underground features such as streams. Evidence also survives telling us the names of ancient and medieval Londoners, what jobs they did, and where they were from.

Where's Lvndonia? It sounds familiar but I can't quite place it.

FUN FACT
LVNDONIA is the Latin name for London. It appears on lots of medieval coins.

An example of a Roman inscription

VLPIVS SILVANVS
EMERITVS LEG II AVG
VOTVM SOLVIT FACTVS
ARAVSIONE

A Roman River

The Thames is one of the oldest place names still in use in Britain. The river was given the name Tamesis by the Roman general Julius Caesar.

Meanwhile, we know the names of over a hundred Roman Londoners from inscriptions, tombstones and graffiti, including an interesting character called Fortunata, whose name appears on a wax tablet. Fortunata was a female slave from Gaul (now France) who was sold in London's slave market, with the description "guaranteed healthy and not likely to run away".

The inscription on the right was found at the Temple of Mithras. Translated, it means: "Ulpius Silvanus, veteran soldier of the Second Augustan Legion, in honouring a vow, makes this altar after having a vision".

Saxon Villages

Place names give useful clues about where the Saxons lived in and around London. Old Saxon villages close to the centre of town include Kensington, Paddington, Islington, Fulham and Stepney. The Saxon Gillingas tribe lived near what is now Ealing, while Barking gets its name from another Saxon tribe, the Berecingas.

How many of these can you find around London? →

> **SAXON PLACE NAMES**
> eccles- = church
> -ham = homestead
> -tun or -ton = village
>
> **VIKING PLACE NAMES**
> kir- = church
> -by = homestead or village
> -gat = road or way

> London Bridge is falling down,
> Falling down, falling down.
> London Bridge is falling down,
> My fair lady.

A Famous Bridge

Have you ever wondered what the famous London Bridge nursery rhyme is about? Think back to the chronicle about King Sweyn and you'll remember Olaf Haroldson's soldiers pulling down the bridge to stop Sweyn's men getting across. Many people think the nursery rhyme may have its origins in that story. Grateful Londoners showed their thanks by naming six churches after Olaf, such as St Olav's in Hart Street.

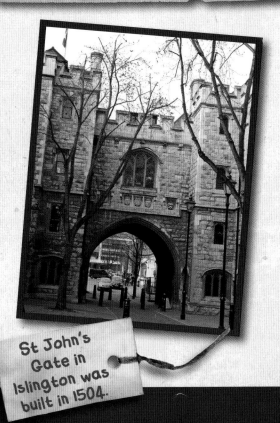

St John's Gate in Islington was built in 1504.

Friars and Gates

None of the seven medieval gates survive today but they live on in the names of areas of today's London. For example Ludgate, Newgate and Cripplegate are all named after the old medieval gates. Crutched Friars and Houndsditch also have medieval names.

Knightsbridge, once a medieval village, takes its name from a bridge which once crossed the Westbourne River. The story goes that two knights once fought here.

Lying in Ruins

Thomas knows he should get back to the monastery kitchens but his feet are rooted to the spot in fear. The king's men are breaking into the monastery! Thomas heard about a similar attack on a nearby abbey where the soldiers marched in and grabbed any treasures they could lay their hands on. Will they do the same here? What will remain of the monastery by the end of the day? Will he lose his job? Thomas is frightened.

Hampton Court was given to Henry VIII as a gift by Cardinal Wolsey in 1528.

A Tudor King

London became one of the biggest and most important cities in Europe during the reign of the Tudors. The first Tudor, Henry VII, came to power at the end of the Wars of the Roses, fought between the rival families of Lancaster and York.

Henry VII's son, Henry VIII, broke from the Catholic Church and made himself head of the new Church of England. He then began to tear down, or 'dissolve', London's monasteries and abbeys. He took their treasures and sold off their lands. Many buildings were left in ruins. Others became sites for grand houses belonging to the king's courtiers. The king grabbed large chunks of land for himself to hunt on. These later became Hyde Park, Regent's Park and Richmond Park.

A Golden Era

Henry VIII's daughter, Mary I, wanted to make England Catholic again. She had over 200 Protestants burned to death at Smithfield. When her Protestant sister, Elizabeth I, came to the throne, hundreds of Catholics were hanged from the gallows at Tyburn, near to where the Marble Arch is today.

Despite the religious unrest, Elizabeth's reign was a golden era for London. Thanks to English explorers such as Sir Walter Raleigh and Sir Francis Drake, London became a global trading centre. The Royal Exchange was built to provide a place where bankers and merchants could do business. Hampton Court, which had been Henry VIII's favourite palace, was one of the most magnificent palaces in Europe.

I'm off to find the City of Gold!

SPOT THIS!

The Golden Hinde in Southwark is a replica of the ship sailed by explorer Sir Francis Drake.

Shakespeare's Globe is a reconstruction of the original theatre which was built in 1599.

Growing Fast

Skilled workers flocked to London from elsewhere in England and abroad throughout the Tudor period. New streets sprang up in the fields around the old city to house the growing population. Rich Londoners built large dwellings while houses for the poor were often badly built.

For entertainment, people liked to visit taverns, watch bear-baiting and cock-fights, or enjoy a play at outdoor theatres such as the Globe or the Rose.

...1588 SPANISH ARMADA DEFEATED...1598 FIRST LONDON GUIDEBOOK IS PRINTED...

25

In Tudor London, people had to make their own fun. After a long day at work, many people simply went to bed when it got dark. The time for entertainment was on a Sunday or Saint's day, when there was often a big public event.

Here a young girl, Anne, describes a family trip to a public execution at Tower Hill. Over 70,000 people were executed in Henry VIII's reign.

The hours leading up to the execution are like a carnival. It's busy and noisy.

I don't really like all the blood, but my father always likes to get a good view. He makes us queue up the night before to make sure we get one of the best places. I cling to my mother's cloak to make sure I don't get swept away in the crowd.

While we're waiting there's lots to see and do. My brothers enjoy the jugglers and acrobats. I prefer the songs sung by the minstrels. There are cartloads of tasty nibbles: dried raisins, hazelnuts, blackberry pies, oysters and mussels.

When it's time for the actual execution, you never know what will happen. Last year, Lady Margaret Pole was chased around the chopping block by the axeman. Father nearly split his sides laughing!

A plaque near Marble Arch marks the spot where about 50,000 people were hanged at the Tyburn Tree gallows.

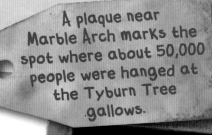
THE SITE OF TYBURN TREE

FUN FACT
The Tudor alphabet had only 24 letters. The letters 'u' and 'v' were the same letter, as were 'i' and 'j'.

I'm a Yeoman Warder and this is my dress uniform for special occasions.

What's a Yeoman Warder?

Top Five Facts

1. Yeoman Warders are guards at the Tower of London.
2. They're nicknamed 'Beefeaters' because they may have once received beef as part of their pay.
3. Their uniform has changed very little since Tudor times.
4. Yeomen Warders wear a blue uniform for everyday duties.
5. Moira Cameron became the first female Beefeater in 2007.

How do we know?

Many Tudor paintings survive, showing us how people looked in Tudor times. A wide variety of other objects also exists, such as mugs, candlesticks and shoes.

Around this time, the first maps of London were being drawn, showing the new streets and the changing shape of the city. Sadly, many of London's Tudor buildings were destroyed in the Great Fire of 1666, so it's hard to get a real sense of what the city was like.

All that remains of the great monasteries are the names they gave to areas of London, such as Greyfriars and Blackfriars. However, a few Tudor palaces in the suburbs, such as Hampton Court and Eltham Palace, are still standing. Henry built several deer parks so he could enjoy hunting in the capital. You can still see deer in Richmond Park, in south London.

London's population mushroomed from 75,000 people in 1500 to 500,000 by 1660.

Plague and Fire!

A young woman runs through the city streets. Though it's the middle of the afternoon, the plague has turned London into a ghost town. The markets and churches are closed. Many of the houses she passes are marked with a red cross, a sign there's a victim inside. The woman hurries on, hoping to find a plague doctor for her son.

Mr Fawkes, do you remember the 5th of November?

When my Gunpowder Plot failed, people in London celebrated by lighting bonfires.

Civil War

The 17th century was a troubled time for London. Londoners were terrified of a Catholic plot to destroy the city, after Guy Fawkes's failed attempt blow up King James I inside the Houses of Parliament on 5th November, 1605.

Then, in the 1640s, England was torn apart by a civil war fought between James's son, Charles I, and Parliament, led by Oliver Cromwell. The king lost the war, and was beheaded in London in 1649. After this, Cromwell ran the country for several years. He was a Puritan – a strict Protestant – who banned sports, dancing and even Christmas decorations! Londoners celebrated when Charles II was restored to the throne in 1660.

Noisy and Dirty

The old centre of London was a horrid place to live. The city was wrapped in a choking blanket of smoke and sulphur fumes from industries such as leather works and soap-making. The narrow streets were clogged with carts, coaches and herds of cattle and pigs brought to the city for slaughter. Piles of steaming dung lay everywhere, and ashes and dust were constantly thrown into the streets. Meanwhile, the Thames was full of floating corpses and waste. At low tide, it stank horribly!

TUDOR
1485–1603

STUART
1603–1714

GEORGIAN
1714–1837

VICTORIAN
1837–1901

MODERN
TIMES
1901–NOW

Destruction!

In 1665, rats on trading ships brought the 'Great Plague' to London. Rich people left town and everyone else hid indoors. Even so, the disease spread fast. Bodies soon piled up on the streets. By the end of the year, over 100,000 people had died.

The next year, in 1666, a small fire that started accidentally turned into a giant blaze that raged for four days. Most of the city inside the walls was burned down. Though few died in the fire, 100,000 people were made homeless. Many of London's finest buildings were destroyed, including St Paul's Cathedral and the Guildhall.

SPOT THIS!

The Monument was built in memory of the Great Fire. Can you spot this at the top of the Monument?

FUN FACT

An army of rats helped to spread the plague. Even today, supposedly you are never more than 2 metres away from a rat in London!

Finished in 1714, St Paul's is still a London landmark today.

London is Rebuilt

London soon rose from the ashes. Architect Sir Christopher Wren designed the magnificent new St Paul's Cathedral and over 50 other churches. Several splendid new theatres were also built, including the Theatre Royal, Drury Lane.

When Charles II moved to St James's Palace in Westminster, many rich Londoners moved to the West End to be near him. They lived in grand new squares with gatekeepers to keep out unwanted flocks of sheep, traders and beggars.

By 1700, London was the largest city in Europe, with a wide mix of peoples. Jewish, Irish and Italian workers living in East London were joined by a wave of Protestant refugees from France.

...1666 THE GREAT FIRE OF LONDON...1694 BANK OF LONDON IS FOUNDED...

29

CELT
500 BC

ROMAN
AD 43–410

ANGLO-
SAXON
AD 450–
1066

VIKING
AD 865–
1066

MEDIEVAL
TIMES
1066–1485

In the early hours of 2nd September, 1666, a fire broke out in the house of baker Thomas Farriner in the heart of the old city. A strong wind swept the fire quickly across town, and soon the streets were packed with crowds of terrified Londoners desperate to escape the flames. Here a young Londoner, Daniel, describes the chaos in his diary.

The whole sky is lit up and I can hear explosions in the distance.

This engraving from 1666 shows the Great Fire of London from the south bank of the Thames.

By the afternoon, the orange and yellow flames were shooting high into the air. The timber houses made a hideous noise as they crackled and burned. People stayed in their homes as long as they could, fleeing at the very last moment.

In the streets, people and horses were panicking. It was very scary and the blocked roads made it impossible for the fire-fighting carts to get through.

My father found a man with a cart to carry our most precious belongings. By nightfall, we finally made it to the safe, open fields. I could hear explosions in the distance. An army officer told me that soldiers and sailors were using gunpowder to knock down houses and stop the fire from spreading. If this doesn't work, what will be left of our noble city?

E. de brandt van London, op den 12. 13. 14. 15. en 16 September Anno 1666.

The poor pigeons were loth [unwilling] to leave their houses, but hovered about the windows and balconies, till some of them burned their wings and fell down.

I wrote my diaries in a type of shorthand that was quick to write. I only used a few full words such as people's names.

Samuel Pepys (pronounced 'Peeps')

A quote from Mr Pepys about the Great Fire

A run of several hot, dry summers meant that London's houses caught fire easily in 1666.

How do we know?

The Great Fire destroyed around four-fifths of London. Plans were created for a new grid of straight streets but London was rebuilt using the old winding streets and alleys. Apart from the churches, few of the buildings rebuilt after the fire survive today, though some were still around long enough to be photographed in Victorian times. Most of the squares that sprang up in West London at the time are still landmarks, such as Soho and Leicester Squares.

By the 17th century, there were all sorts of written records, including detailed diaries written by Londoners such as Samuel Pepys and John Evelyn. The *Daily Courant*, perhaps the world's first regular daily newspaper, was first printed in London's Fleet Street in 1702. A print by Wenceslaus Holler shows the parts of London that were destroyed by the fire.

CELT 500 BC	ROMAN AD 43–410	ANGLO-SAXON AD 450–1066	VIKING AD 865–1066	MEDIEVAL TIMES 1066–1485

Boom Town!

This evening it seems as if the whole city has gathered at the Vauxhall Gardens. It's a maze of walks, flowerbeds and trees. Visitors can spot the latest fashions, catch up on gossip and maybe even catch sight of the Prince Regent himself. There are hot air balloons, fireworks, concerts and tightrope walkers. Later, everyone will dine in the open air. All for just one shilling!

Luxury and Slavery

Four King Georges ruled from 1714 to 1830, lending their name to the Georgian period of British history. During this time, Britain became a very powerful nation, thanks to its growing empire in India and America. Goods were shipped to London from all over the world. If you had money, you could buy anything and everything in the capital.

Hundreds of small factories and workshops made luxury goods such as pottery, clocks, silk cloth and furniture. London's merchants also grew wealthy on the cruel sugar and slave trades. Nearly 750,000 African slaves passed through London, many on their way to plantations in the Caribbean and America.

> With its balls, banquets and fashion, London is the place to be!

Spreading Out

For much of the 18th century, London was a boom town. Leafy squares and broad streets sprang up across the West End, a home for doctors, lawyers, army captains and merchants. Rows of fine houses also appeared along the roads out of London, in areas such as Kensington, Chelsea and Knightsbridge.

London Bridge was cleared of buildings because they weren't making enough money in rent for the city. This helped to ease traffic on the bridge. The old Roman walls circling the City of London were torn down. Two new bridges were built at Westminster and Blackfriars, opening up new suburbs such as Camberwell south of the river.

TUDOR 1485–1603	STUART 1603–1714	GEORGIAN 1714–1837	VICTORIAN 1837–1901	MODERN TIMES 1901–NOW

Made in 1757, this state coach is used in the Lord Mayor's Parade.

The Square Mile

London also became a world banking centre. Most banks were found in the 'Square Mile', the old City of London centred around the Bank of England. Bankers and merchants did business in the coffee houses nearby, especially in Exchange Alley, the site of London's stock exchange. Here investors bought shares in a company, hoping to make a profit if it did well. In 1720, thousands of investors were ruined after shares in the South Sea Company tumbled in value.

In Fashion

London's prosperity continued into the 19th century, thanks partly to victory over France and Napoleon in 1815. Many old buildings were torn down and roads were widened. Streets were now lit by gas lights and iron water pipes brought fresh water into the city.

Under the Prince Regent, who later became King George IV, London became a centre of fashion. At its heart was a smart new district created by architect John Nash. This included Regent's Street, Regent's Park and nearby streets and crescents lined with town houses and villas. Other London landmarks such as Piccadilly Circus, Trafalgar Square and the National Gallery were also built at this time.

King George III

George III had the nickname 'Farmer George'. He liked to visit farms, dressed in farmer's clothes.

FUN FACT
The British Museum first opened to the public in 1759. Today it is famous for its Egyptian mummies and Ancient Greek sculptures.

COOL!

Rich and Poor

Georgian London was like two cities living side by side. The rich lived in magnificent houses with glass windows, chandeliers, sofas and mirrors; they ate with forks from china plates. On the other side of town, the poor lived on a diet of bread, cabbages and beans and ate from wooden or pewter bowls. Their homes were cramped, overcrowded and often damp. Crime was a big problem – even King George II was robbed while out for an afternoon stroll.

Doesn't this thing go any faster?

Sedan chairs were used to carry rich people around.

Designed in 1828, the Marble Arch has three small rooms inside it!

A Place for Fun

There was lots for 18th-century wealthy Londoners to enjoy: balls, concerts, books and banquets. Gatherings known as salons were a place for polite conversation and musical performances. Great artists were drawn to the capital, such as composer George Frederick Handel, writer Samuel Johnson and the painters Thomas Gainsborough and Joshua Reynolds.

New types of shops grew up to cope with the growing demand for tea and coffee and sweet puddings. There were even jelly houses! Crowds flocked to open-air pleasure gardens such as the New Spring Gardens in Vauxhall and Ranelagh Gardens in Chelsea.

Wild London

Eighteenth-century London was known for its grim prisons and its dirty streets with raggedy children. Poor slum areas such as Holborn and Limehouse were a labyrinth of dark, tangled alleys. Cheap gin was easier to get hold of than clean water. Many poor Londoners drank themselves to death. Workhouses set up to help the poorest were little more than prisons where workers toiled in filthy conditions. Anyone who got into debt was flung into prison.

Today's criminal court at the Old Bailey stands on the site of Newgate prison.

The Gordon Riots

Georgian London was a violent place. Mobs of weavers and other badly paid workers often took their anger out on foreigners. Meanwhile a gang of rich young men known as the 'Mohawks' poked passers-by with swords just for fun. In 1780, during the Gordon Riots, 60,000 Londoners took to the streets to protest against a new law giving more rights to Catholics. For six days angry mobs went on the rampage, attacking Newgate prison, the law courts and private homes belonging to judges. In the end, 10,000 soldiers were brought in to stop the riots.

Buckingham Palace was originally built for the Duke of Buckingham.

Over 250 people died in the Gordon Riots. Britain came very close to a revolution.

SPOT THIS!

George III bought Buckingham Palace in 1761. Can you spot this Royal Crest on the gates?

Fighting Crime

FUN FACT
The Bow Street Runners were nicknamed 'Raw Lobsters' because of their red vests!

Until the 18th century, London was guarded by its citizens. They took turns to patrol the streets on foot. In the 1750s, Henry Fielding set up the Bow Street Runners, London's first paid police officers. If caught, criminals were given harsh punishments such as being whipped, burned with a red-hot iron, or dragged through the streets. In the 1800s, thousands of criminals were shipped to America and later Australia.

In Georgian London, the shopkeepers of the West End used all sorts of tactics to attract customers. Some fitted large plate glass windows to show off their goods. Other novelties included arcades, covered shopping areas that could be enjoyed on rainy days, and bazaars, shops that provided entertainment. Here a young girl, Jane, writes to a relative describing an exciting shopping trip with her brother, Thomas.

A mongoose in a shopping arcade! What a strange surprise!

15th June, 1823

Dear Great Aunt Maud,

You won't believe the things I saw today! We were walking along Oxford Street and Miss Groves, our governess, was suffering badly in the heat. So Tom and I persuaded her to take us to the Pantheon Bazaar.

Passing through the porch, we entered a room filled with sculptures, leafy plants and a fountain. Miss Groves was happy to be away from the smell of the horses on the street!

Walking up a flight of steps we found ourselves in an open gallery with a beautiful roof made of coloured glass. It was a shopper's paradise, with everything from gloves and furs to jewellery and glass ornaments.

Miss Groves wanted to take a look at the children's bookshop and toy shop, but as soon as Tom heard a squawking parrot we ran off to see the pet shops. There were monkeys, snakes and even a mongoose. I'm quite sure you don't see many of those in Dorset!

Your loving niece,

Jane

FUN FACT
Burlington Arcade in Piccadilly opened in 1818. It was patrolled by security guards known as 'beadles' who wore top hats and tailcoats.

A famous cartoon by Hogarth

How do we know?

In 1808, a poet called Robert Southey described London's shops in one of his letters. He wrote that there was "a shop to every house, street after street and mile after mile...such a display of splendour". Other interesting written sources include newspapers such as *The Spectator*, the famous diaries by James Boswell and the novels of Jane Austen and Henry Fielding.

Cartoonists William Hogarth and James Gillray drew scenes of daily life at the time. Hogarth's cartoons showed the dark side of London life in the 18th century, such as the dangers of drinking and gambling.

Fine Georgian buildings survive in many parts of London, for example those in Henrietta Street near Covent Garden. The nearby alleyway of Goodwin's Court still has curved windows and gas lamps, like it did in Georgian times.

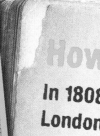

The person who has not pleasure in a good novel must be intolerably stupid.

Jane Austen

By 1828 there were over 50 shops in Burlington Arcade.

What's in a Name?

A lot of building work was carried out in London after the Great Fire and during Georgian times. In fact, much of the city you see today was built in the 17th and 18th centuries. Bedford Square, for example, is one of the best-preserved Georgian squares in London. Some buildings are named after the person who built or paid for them. But other placenames have interesting stories behind them...

How fair is Mayfair? And isn't Piccadilly silly!

Silly Piccadilly

Piccadilly is thought to have gained its name from Piccadilly Hall, built in about 1612 by a tailor called Robert Baker. The tailor named his home after piccadils – small, stiff collars worn by English gentlemen at that time.

Before this, Stoke Newington became a popular pitstop for people travelling north from London in medieval and Tudor times. Its name means 'new town in the wood'.

According to legend there was an old lady called Sarah Whitehead who sat on Threadneedle Street every day for 25 years. She was mourning the death of her brother, who had worked at the Bank of England and was executed for forgery. Today the 'Old Lady of Threadneedle Street' is a nickname for the Bank of England.

Do you know the story behind the Bank of England's nickname?

TUDOR 1485–1603	STUART 1603–1714	GEORGIAN 1714–1837	VICTORIAN 1837–1901	MODERN TIMES 1901– NOW

Tally ho, Soho!

Soho supposedly got its name in the 17th century when the area was mainly fields. Hunting parties shouted "So ho!" as they rode through the fields. Pall Mall also got its name around this time. It comes from a French game called 'paille mail' that was played on lawns, like croquet.

Bleeding Heart Yard is a cobbled courtyard in Hatton Garden. The bleeding heart behind the name belonged to Lady Hatton who was murdered in the courtyard in 1662 having just hosted her annual winter ball. Meanwhile, the posh district of Mayfair is named after a rowdy Hyde Park festival from the late 17th century. It was a magnet for pickpockets and gamblers.

Lady Hatton? Murdered?! Where?

The Grand old Duke of York
he had ten thousand men.
He marched them up to the
top of the hill,
And he marched them down again.

Do you know the tune to this rhyme?

Who's That?

An obelisk stands near the Mall in remembrance of the Duke of York. It's been there since 1834 and you can see a statue of the duke himself standing at the top.

Seven Sisters

Have you heard of the Seven Sisters? It's an area in London but it's not named after seven human sisters, as you might think. The seven sisters were actually elm trees, planted in a circle.

Meanwhile, Greenwich became a household name when Greenwich Mean Time was adopted across the world. This came about after the British Nautical Almanac was produced at the Royal Observatory in the 17th century. The almanac showed charts of the stars throughout the seasons of the year.

Who's that up there? It's the grand old Duke of York.

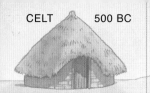
The Great Exhibition

Already thrilled by the giant dinosaur models in the gardens outside, a group of schoolboys stare in wonder at the 'Crystal Palace'. All around are mechanical marvels from every part of the British Empire, from steam engines to the world's largest organ. Later there is going to be a circus! The boys feel very proud. It's 1851, and the Great Exhibition shows why their city, London, leads the world.

Industrial London

When Queen Victoria came to the throne in 1837, the Industrial Revolution was already in full swing. Machines whirred and great factories belched out smoke. London's brewing, engineering and shipbuilding industries all thrived. The capital was the hub of the largest and richest empire on the planet.

The Great Exhibition of 1851 was a chance for Britain to show off its industrial achievements. Held in the Crystal Palace in Hyde Park, the exhibition was viewed by more than 6 million visitors from all over the world. Objects on display included looms, tapestries, furniture and all kinds of interesting new inventions.

The Natural History Museum, V&A and Science Museum were built using profits from the Great Exhibition.

The Railway Age

The coming of the railways in the 1840s transformed London. Poor neighbourhoods were torn down to build stations, tracks and shunting yards. Within 20 years, London was linked to the rest of the country by a network of railways. By the end of Victoria's reign, the capital was also home to ocean-going steamships, a modern postal service and the electric telegraph. A network of over 380 trams allowed millions of Londoners to travel quickly and cheaply about town.

The world's first underground railway, the Metropolitan, opened in 1863. Known by Londoners as the 'Tube', it had 100 kilometres of track within 12 years.

Changing the Guard began when Queen Victoria moved into Buckingham Palace in 1837.

New Docks

A new docks complex was built in the East End to cope with the growing trade with Britain's colonies. London's banks also grew larger – and richer – and office blocks sprang up in the City. In Victorian times, London was also making more money from visitors and tourism, as it does today.

SPOT THIS! Finished in 1843, Nelson's Column has four bronze scenes at its base. Can you spot this one?

Spreading Out

Trams and railway lines allowed middle-class workers to commute into town from areas outside the old city, known as suburbs. Meanwhile most poor Londoners stayed in the crumbling city centre. London grew rapidly, spreading outwards into new districts such as Islington, Paddington and Lambeth.

By 1900, there were 6 million people living in the capital. Many of the newcomers were refugees from Ireland following the Great Famine. Thousands of Jews fleeing from persecution in Eastern Europe moved into the East End, along with families from Britain's colonies in China and southern Asia.

Slumming it

For all its wealth and technology, 19th century London was also a city of terrible poverty. Millions lived in overcrowded, horrific slums. In poor areas the streets were filled with beggars, barefooted street sellers and badly fed labourers who worked long and hard for little pay. The dirty conditions and lack of clean water made London the 'capital of cholera' (a deadly disease). The air people breathed was often foggy with the smoke from coal fires. To add to the chaos, cattle were still driven through London to the bloody slaughterhouses of Smithfield.

Many of London's cemeteries were built by the Victorians. This is Brompton Cemetery.

After Prince Albert died in 1861, Queen Victoria wore black for the rest of her life.

FUN FACT
Beatrix Potter borrowed names for some of her characters from gravestones in Brompton Cemetery, such as Mr McGregor and Mr Nutkin.

Having Fun

There were few pleasures for poor Londoners. Tobacco had arrived from America in Tudor times and, by the 17th century, men, women and children all over London were smoking. Public houses, or 'pubs', were also very popular in Victorian times. Working-class Londoners went to music halls to watch singers, magicians and other entertainers. Most were just a large room at the back of a pub, but some music halls turned into large venues with seats for over 2,000 people.

The Great Stink

For centuries, sewage dumped in London's streets simply flowed into the Thames. As the city grew larger, the problem only got worse. In the hot summer of 1858, the smell from the river was so bad it was known as the 'Great Stink'. Within days Parliament voted to end the problem once and for all. The brilliant engineer Sir Joseph Bazalgette solved the stench by building a giant sewer system for London. He saved the lives of thousands of Londoners by cleaning up the city's water supply. However, London streets were still filled with manure from horses.

Who the Dickens is this?

One of my novels, Oliver Twist, is set in the slums of Victorian London.

This house in Doughty Street was once the home of Charles Dickens.

The Peelers

Victorian Londoners were plagued by burglars and gangs of pickpockets, while criminal gangs fought each other on the streets. Sir Robert Peel decided it was time London had a modern police force, and in 1829 he set up the Metropolitan Police. Though many criminals used guns and other weapons, its officers were armed with only a truncheon. They were called 'Bobbies' or 'Peelers' after their founder. A few years later, Scotsman James Braidwood set up a modern firefighting service for the capital.

SPOT THIS!

Look out for this statue of Sir Robert Peel in Parliament Square.

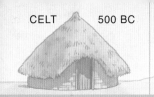

Poor children in Victorian London were expected to work long hours from a very young age. Though the work was often dirty and dangerous, they were paid very little. Some children worked in factories while others ran errands, swept the roads or sold matches or flowers. Boys were also used to sweep chimneys, even after a law in 1832 banned this.

In this imaginary account, a former sweep named Billy tells us what the job was like.

I was six years old when the sweep master came. He paid my father so that I would work for him. I had to scramble up inside the chimney to scrape and brush the soot away. It was very dark and scary.

By the time I was finished, I'd be covered in soot. My elbows and knees would be bleeding from all the cuts and grazes. My master simply rubbed the wounds with salt water then put me back to work.

The chimneys were often narrow and twisted. Some of my friends got stuck and were found dead. My master wasn't the worst. Some of them lit fires underneath their sweeps to make them get on with the job!

Please don't shout at me, Miss. I'm only six.

Tower Bridge is the result of a Victorian design competition! It was finished in 1894.

Westminster Palace is another name for the Houses of Parliament.

Queen Victoria in her Diamond Jubilee Parade

This is a Victorian camera. The leather bellows were moved in or out to change the focus.

How do we know?

Many of London's buildings today were built in Victorian times, from the terraces of houses in suburbs like Clapham to great buildings such as the Royal Albert Hall and the Houses of Parliament.

From the 1850s onwards, cameras were increasingly common, and photographs provide a fantastic record of what Victorian London looked like, from tram-filled streets to family portraits. There's also a mass of written evidence from maps and books to menus and tram timetables.

From 1801, every ten years the British government collected information about everyone in England, known as a census. Comparing information in different censuses can tell us a lot about how London was changing.

London changed rapidly in Victorian times.

45

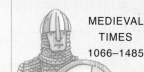
A Restless Place

The girl grips her mother's hand as they make their way to Hyde Park with the Suffragettes. Crowds line London's streets as the protestors walk past holding banners. Brass bands play marching music as the parade snakes its way towards the park. Here 300,000 people gather to listen to speeches demanding 'Votes for Women'. London has seen many protests over the years, but nothing like this!

FUN FACT
London hosted the Olympic Games for the first time in 1908 at a new stadium built in White City.

The Votes for Women campaign was organized by Suffragettes. Some chained themselves to railings outside government buildings!

Imperial City

When Queen Victoria's son Edward VII was crowned in 1901, London was the proud capital city of a huge empire stretching as far as Canada and Australia. Several large building projects made the city even grander. The Mall and Admiralty Arch created a dramatic approach to Buckingham Palace. Waterloo Station was rebuilt with a majestic new entrance.

London was also a centre for change, as working men and women demanding the vote took to its streets in protest. Problems such as crime, bad housing and disease among the poor remained. But the new London County Council tried to clear the worst slums as well as building schools, libraries and public baths.

Going Electric!

New technology brought big changes to the capital. In 1888, Electric Avenue in Brixton became the first shopping street to be lit by electricity. In 1904, London had its first motor bus. Electric trams were also increasingly common, and dozens of power stations were built to supply electricity to the capital. The first electric cookers also appeared, though most homes did not have electricity until the 1920s.

The early 1900s saw the arrival of big department stores such as Harrods.

Tourism took off, with large hotels such as the Ritz and the Waldorf being built.

SPOT THIS!

Built in 1912, Admiralty Arch has its very own nose! You can find it on the inside of one of the arches.

The Leisure Age

New venues sprang up all over London in the early 20th century, especially in the West End. The London Palladium was the largest of 60 new theatres. From the 1890s onwards, dozens of cinemas also appeared. Improved transport brought more people into the West End. By now many Londoners were better off and could afford to head into town to shop, go to a restaurant, or see a film.

But this wasn't always a happy time for Londoners. During World War One (1914–1918), German airships dropped bombs on London, killing 670 people. While millions of British men went to fight in Europe, back home in London women helped out by working in arms factories or driving buses.

Today we're used to having music all around us. In Edwardian London, you might hear a barrel organ on a street corner or a band playing in the park. But most music was made simply by people singing or whistling on buses or in shops.

Londoners loved going to one of the many music halls. It was a cheap night out, and the audience enjoyed singing along with the performers. Here an imaginary girl, Marie, describes a trip to the music hall.

If you've never had a roasted chestnut you simply MUST try one.

23rd November, 1910

We all got very excited as we queued up for our tickets at the Tivoli. It was bitterly cold outside, so I had goosebumps all over by the time we got in.

Inside it was lovely and warm. We managed to get a row of seats so we could all sit together, with Gran at one end and the twins at the other.

There were lots of different acts, from puppets and fire-eaters to jugglers and magicians. My brother, Eddie, loves comedians and cycling acts, while Mum and I prefer singing along to tunes like "I Do Like to be Beside the Seaside" and "Daisy Bell".

It was a great night and, after the show, Dad bought us a bag of roast chestnuts. Yum!

The next day, Mum borrowed a copy of her favourite tune from the night before. We all stood around the piano and had a right old knees-up!

Edwardian times were named after Edward VII who ruled from 1901 to 1910.

48

TUDOR
1485–1603

STUART
1603–1714

GEORGIAN
1714–1837

VICTORIAN
1837–1901

MODERN
TIMES
1901–
NOW

MRS. PANKHURST AT TRAFALGAR SQUARE INVITING THE AUDIENCE TO "RUSH"
THE HOUSE OF COMMONS ON OCTOBER 13.
The National Women's Social and Political Union,
4, Clements Inn, W.C.

This photo shows leading Suffragette, Emmeline Pankhurst, addressing crowds in Trafalgar Square in about 1910.

How do we know?

A few short films survive showing the hustle and bustle of London life in the early 20th century. The pavements are crowded with men in suits and caps, and women in long skirts and feathered hats holding parasols.

There are clips of film on the Internet showing pedestrians dodging horse-drawn carriages in Pall Mall, Petticoat Lane market and demonstrations in Trafalgar Square. Most films were silent until the 1920s.

The early 1900s also saw the arrival of the first phonographs, which recorded sounds on wax cylinders. We can still listen to recordings of people talking, singing or telling jokes in Edwardian times.

The words of many music-hall songs describe events in the news and can tell us how ordinary people felt about them.

There was lots of fun to be had in Edwardian London.

49

What's in a Name?

Many new buildings and streets grew up in Victorian London. Several of these were named after members of the Royal family, particularly Queen Victoria and her husband Prince Albert. The queen believed that outdoor space was important for people's health, which led to many parks being built. Can you think of a Victoria Park near you?

> One has to wonder – why are there so many Victoria Parks around?

The Prince himself

A Princely Place

Prince Albert worked closely with Queen Victoria to help and advise her during her reign. After Albert's death, the queen chose to name the Royal Albert Hall after him. The V&A Museum is another example of a famous building that honours the royal couple. Even two of the embankments built to house London's new drains along the Thames were named the Victoria and Albert Embankments.

Proms concerts have been held at the Royal Albert Hall every summer since 1941.

Pubs and Pearls

Several Victorian pubs gave their name to underground stations such as the Elephant and Castle, Royal Oak and the Angel, Islington. Meanwhile, Pearly Kings and Queens appeared in Victorian times. Today the suits with rows of shiny buttons are still worn by Cockneys to collect money for charity.

FUN FACT
Traditionally, Cockneys are Londoners born within the sound of the bells of the church of St Mary-le-Bow.

A pair of pearly queens!

UNDERGROUND

There's not a real elephant and castle at the station, you know.

Plates of Meat

Rhyming slang was probably invented by London's street-traders in Victorian times. They could chat without their customers or the police knowing what they were saying. Do you recognize some of the common phrases on the right?

Rhyming slang	Meaning
Apples and pears	Stairs
Barnet Fair	Hair
Plates of meat	Feet
Butcher's hook	Look
Peckham Rye	Tie
Hampstead Heath	Teeth
Whistle and flute	Suit

Evacuate!

All of a sudden, Charlie and Dot feel very shy. Earlier today they were escorted to the train station by their teacher with lots of other children. They crowded onto the platform, each carrying a gas mask, sandwiches and apples for the journey, and a bag of clothes. Then they had a long journey to this strange place in the country. Dot is worried she might never see Mum and Dad again. Charlie puts an arm around her. At least they weren't split up like some brothers and sisters.

Before the War

There was a new mood in the city during the 1920s. Londoners headed up to the West End to dance the night away, listen to jazz, or watch a movie. Giant crowds enjoyed football matches or horse racing. In 1922, the BBC broadcast its first radio show.

In the 1930s, many homes had cars, cookers and fridges for the first time, and some of the old inner city slums were replaced by council flats. On the streets, electric lighting and motor vehicles replaced the old gas lighting and horse-drawn vehicles. More and more women could enjoy fashion. They wore cheap dresses that copied the styles worn by movie stars.

London's famous red telephone boxes first appeared in 1929.

FUN FACT
Though evacuees missed their homes, many enjoyed the country. Some had never seen cows, or apples growing from trees.

I'm an air-raid warden. It's my job to help people during an attack by enemy bombers.

Air Raids

In 1939, Britain declared war on Germany after Hitler invaded Poland. Fearing an attack, 700,000 Londoners, left, or 'evacuated', the city. Most evacuees were children.

In September 1940, German planes dropped hundreds of bombs on the East End. The nightly air raids, known as the 'Blitz', went on for eight months. Thousands of Londoners slept in underground stations for safety. Sadly, not everyone was safe from the bombs and 80,000 people were killed. Over a million homes were destroyed.

In 1944, London came under attack again. First was the V-1, a robot 'flying bomb'. Then came the V-2 rocket. This flew so fast no one could see or hear it coming.

While sheltering in a London Underground station, these children met the King and queen!

Blitz Spirit

Though many Londoners tried to live life as normal during the war, it wasn't easy. To buy clothes and basic foods such as meat, eggs and milk, you needed a ration book. This system made sure that everybody got a fair share of what was available. Meanwhile people waited anxiously for news from the front. Many received telegrams carrying news of the capture or death of loved ones.

Despite all of this, Londoners had 'Blitz spirit' – they helped one another and tried to stay positive. King George VI and his wife, Queen Elizabeth, made regular visits into the city to boost morale. St Paul's Cathedral survived the bombing and many people felt that, as long as St Paul's was standing, they had a hope of winning the war.

SPOT THIS!

A mural in Cable Street shows a battle in 1936 when East Enders stood up for local Jews to fight Fascism.

Some children stayed in London because their parents refused to have them evacuated. But life during the Blitz was often tough for children living in the city. Here a young girl, Bess, describes what it was like.

Many families listen to the radio every night for news of the war.

Visitors can find out about wartime Britain at the Imperial War Museum.

These days, life is either very boring or very scary. Dad is away fighting, while Mum spends most of the day working in a factory.

After school, a gang of us look for bits of shells or shrapnel. Bombed-out houses are our playgrounds. Sometimes we manage to sneak into one of the cinemas that are still open.

At night, when we hear the wailing sound of the air-raid siren, Mum and I run down to the shelter at the bottom of our garden. You can hear the throb of the German bombers flying overhead, then the terrible crashes and bangs of bombs exploding everywhere.

Worst of all was when a bomb landed in the road opposite. When the sirens gave the 'all clear', we went outside and saw a whole row of houses flattened. Firefighters were doing their best to tackle the blaze and rescue teams were pulling people from the rubble.

Government Air Raid Warning in 1939:

When you hear the warning take cover at once. Remember that most of the injuries in an air raid are caused not by direct hits by bombs but by flying fragments of debris or by bits of shells.

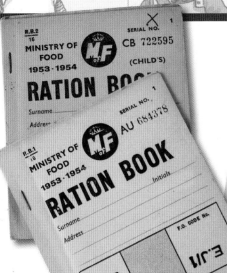

R.B.2
1/6
MINISTRY OF FOOD
1953-1954
RATION BOOK (CHILD'S)
SERIAL NO. CB 722595
Surname..............
Address..............

R.B.1
1/6
MINISTRY OF FOOD
1953-1954
RATION BOOK
SERIAL NO. 1 AU 684378
Initials..............
Surname..............
Address..............
F.O. CODE No.
E.J11
IF FOUND RETURN TO ANY FOOD OFFICE

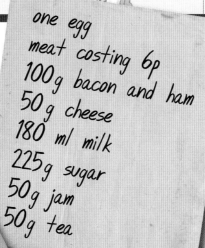

one egg
meat costing 6p
100g bacon and ham
50 g cheese
180 ml milk
225 g sugar
50 g jam
50 g tea

A week's worth of food rations for one adult

War-time gas masks are in great condition because there was never a gas attack.

Many people kept their ration books after the war, giving us plenty of evidence of how rationing worked.

How do we know?

Newspaper and radio reports and the government tried to keep people's spirits up with stories about German planes being shot down or people going to parties and restaurants as normal. But personal records such as diaries, photos, letters, postcards and memoirs reveal how difficult life really was for most people during the war.

There is also some remarkable film footage from the Blitz, some of it in colour, showing burning buildings, people queueing for rations, and children being evacuated.

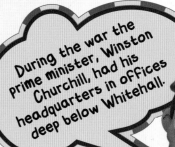

During the war the prime minister, Winston Churchill, had his headquarters in offices deep below Whitehall.

Swinging London

Carnaby Street is crammed with small shops selling the latest colourful fashions. Loud music blares from every doorway, interrupted by the phut-phut of scooters driven by gangs of 'Mods' wearing hooded jackets. Smartly-dressed men in bowler hats on their way to work stroll past a group of long-haired hippies in beads, long flowery dresses and hats. Carnaby Street is the place to be!

New Arrivals

After World War Two, thousands of homes were built to replace those that were destroyed in the Blitz. Many Poles and Italians came to work in London, along with skilled workers invited from former colonies in India, Pakistan and the Caribbean. Over the next 30 years, they were joined by refugees from Vietnam, Greek and Turkish Cypriots, Chinese families from Hong Kong, and many other groups. But some Londoners feared the new arrivals, leading to riots in the Notting Hill district of west London in 1958.

20 million people in Britain watched the coronation of Queen Elizabeth II on television in 1953.

FUN FACT
Not everyone had a TV in the 1950s. Over half the audience of the queen's coronation went to a friend's house to watch television.

...1952 'GREAT SMOG' KILLS THOUSANDS...1958 NOTTING HILL RIOTS...

Rock 'n' Roll

In the 1960s, 'Swinging' London was a very exciting place to live. Fashionable Londoners wore bright colours and mini skirts. They listened to rock 'n' roll and pop groups such as the Beatles. The city was brighter in other ways, thanks to a new law banning smoky fuels and encouraging people to heat their homes with electricity and gas rather than coal fires. Many of the old inner-city slum buildings were replaced with high-rise tower blocks.

All sorts of new fashions appeared in London in the 1960s and '70s.

← What can you see from the London Eye?

Modern London

The boom times returned in the mid-1980s, driven by London's banking and finance industries. Gleaming office blocks sprang up in the docklands and in the old City. By the 1990s, London was a confident global centre again, with a young, mixed population. Tourists flocked to enjoy the capital's sights and sounds. Modern landmarks like the Millennium Dome and the London Eye gave London a new look.

Difficult Times

The 1970s and 1980s were a low point in London's history. A bombing campaign by the IRA brought fear to the city's streets. As the British Empire shrank, London's docks grew quiet. Many factories closed as they couldn't compete with cheap goods made abroad and lots of Londoners lost their jobs. Strikes and protests were common and, in 1981, race riots took place in Brixton.

SPOT THIS! This bridge was built in London to mark the new millennium in 2000. Have you walked over it?

In the 1950s and 1960s, large numbers of immigrants came to London looking for work, changing the city forever. As a result, almost one in five Londoners today have family roots in Africa and south Asia, in countries which used to be part of the British empire.

In this imaginary account, a young boy called Nazmul writes to a family friend in Bradford about Brick Lane, the heart of London's Bangladeshi community.

My brother calls the market 'Banglatown'!

Dear Auntie-ji,

You'd love the crazy markets of Brick Lane. They're full of noise and fantastic smells! Every week it's different, with new stalls appearing under railway bridges, in warehouses and any bit of open space. People sell all sorts of old junk here, from old car radios, books and TV remote controls to crumpled suits and pirate videos.

My favourite part is a street called Club Row, where you can buy birds, goldfish and all sorts of small animals. Opposite the old church, butchers and fruit sellers come up with catchy lines to win customers from their rivals.

If you're peckish, a few stalls nearby sell jellied eels and shellfish, while Sis loves the bagels from the Jewish bakery. Further down are the Lane's curry houses and sweet shops selling sticky desserts.

You must visit us to try some!

Lots of love,
Nazmul

Notting Hill Carnival is one of the world's largest street festivals.

THE DAILY NEWS

8th July, 2005 • Your favourite newspaper

Mayor of London, Ken Livingstone, takes pride in the city of London after yesterday's terrorist bombings:

"In this city 300 languages are spoken and the people that speak them live side by side in harmony… This is a city where you can be yourself as long as you don't harm anyone else. You can live your life as you choose to do rather than as somebody else tells you to do… That, I think, is our strength and that is what the bombers seek to destroy."

↑ Imaginary newspaper article

This dragon is part of Chinese New Year celebrations in London.

Chinatown contains restaurants, souvenir shops, bakeries and other Chinese-run businesses.

Oyez, oyez! Come to London today!

How do we know?

By the 1970s, almost every home in Britain had a television. TV shows can tell us a lot about how people lived, from news reports and interviews to cookery and children's programmes.

Another great source of information comes from stories of people who were alive at the time. This is called oral history and is one of the ways we know about families like Nazmul's. More and more people are doing their own research into their family history. Why not ask your grandparents to tell you about life in London when they were young?

 CELT 500 BC	 ROMAN AD 43–410	ANGLO-SAXON AD 450–1066	 VIKING AD 865–1066	 MEDIEVAL TIMES 1066–1485

Today and Tomorrow

London has come a long way since the Romans arrived 2,000 years ago. We know how it has changed thanks to objects dug from the ground, written records, old maps and paintings and the many historical buildings that survive. So how will people know about today's Londoners in the future?

⬆ The giant dome built to celebrate the millennium is now home to a large indoor arena staging rock and pop concerts. What music will Londoners be listening to in 100 years' time?

Jafaican is a new way of speaking English in London. It mixes Caribbean phrases with old Cockney slang.

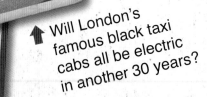

⬆ Will London's famous black taxi cabs all be electric in another 30 years?

⬅ Many scientists predict that global warming will make sea levels rise in the future. So will the Thames Barrier still protect London from floods and high tides in another 50 years?

St Paul's is one of London's best-loved features and even survived the Blitz. Will it dominate the skyline in another 300 years? ➡

⬆ A new stadium at Stratford has been built for the 2012 Olympic games. What new events do you think there will be in another 100 years' time?

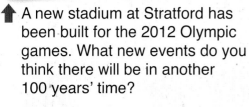

⬅ The 'Gherkin' is built on the site of a building destroyed by a terrorist bomb. What dangers might Londoners face in the future?

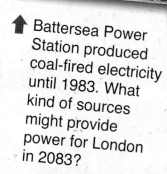

⬆ Battersea Power Station produced coal-fired electricity until 1983. What kind of sources might provide power for London in 2083?

How will they know?

How will future generations know what London was like for us, now? The internet is a great way of recording the present. Photos, blogs and stories from tourists can all spread the word about our wonderful city. Hundreds of years from now someone may be looking at your picture or reading your blog. You're making history!

Glossary

Abbey – a Christian monastery or convent run by an abbot.

AD – a short way of writing the Latin words anno Domini, which mean 'in the year of our Lord', i.e. after the birth of Christ.

Amphitheatre – a round, open-air theatre, surrounded by seats which rise from the centre so everyone can see.

Archaeologist – a person who studies the past by looking at the remains left by people.

BC – a short way of writing 'before the birth of Christ'.

Beefeater – Yeoman Warder or guard of the Tower of London.

Blitz, the – a time during World War Two when Britain was bombed by German planes.

Catholic – a member of the Christian religion that considers the pope to be the head of its church.

Cauldron – a large pot used for boiling.

Charter – a document giving certain authority or rights.

Cholera – a deadly disease caused by filthy water.

Evacuate – having to leave your home and live somewhere else for safety.

Fort – a large, strong building offering support and protection.

Garderobe – a toilet in a medieval building that let the waste fall straight into the street or a moat.

Latin – a language originally spoken in Ancient Rome.

Mammoth – a large extinct elephant with a hairy coat.

Merchant – a person who buys and sells goods in order to make a living.

Monastery – a place where monks live and worship.

Monk – a male member of a religious community that has rules of poverty, chastity and obedience.

Mosaic – a design made up of small pieces of glass or stone.

Pillory – a wooden frame with holes for the head and hands, used for punishment.

Plague (Black Death) – a serious disease that is carried by rats and can be transferred to humans by fleas.

Protestant – a member of the Christian religion that considers the king or queen to be the head of its church.

Rationing – this controlled the amount of food and fuel people could use during World War Two in order to save resources.

Rhyming slang – rhyming phrases used by Londoners.

Sedan chair – a covered chair with poles, enabling it to be carried by one person at the front and one at the back.

Slave – any person who is owned by another. Slaves have no freedom or rights and work for no payment.

Workhouse – a place where poor people could go to live and work when they had no job or home.

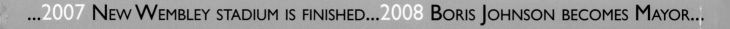

Index

Acknowledgements

The author and publishers would like to thank John Park and Greg Williams at
the City of London Corporation Press Office for their generous help.

The publishers would also like to thank the following people and organizations
for their permission to reproduce material on the following pages:
Front cover: Patrick Wang/Shutterstock, Woodsy007/Shutterstock, photogl/Shutterstock, AKaiser/Shutterstock, Vollchenok/
Shutterstock, Smit/Shutterstock, Philip Lange/Shutterstock; back cover: Hazeelin Hassan/Shutterstock, S.Borisov/Shutterstock,
Val Lawless/Shutterstock; p5: City of London Corporation Press Office; p6: Trish Steel/Geograph; Fishbourne Museum,
Chichester; p7: Lonpicman/Wikipedia; p8: Fishbourne Museum, Chichester; p11: Fishbourne Museum, Chichester;
p12: Steve Daniels/Geograph; p13: Dpaajones/Wikipedia; p14: Peterborough.Chronicle.firstpage-en, User, Geogre/Wikipedia;
p15: York Archaeological Trust, www.jorvik-viking-centre.co.uk; p19: ColsTravel UK/Alamy; www.mikepeel.net/Wikipedia;
p24: Steve Cadman/Wikipedia; p30: Mary Evans Picture Library/GROSVENOR PRINTS; p31: City of London Corporation
Press Office; p37: City of London Corporation Press Office, Andrew Dunn/Wikipedia; p43: Runcorn/Wikipedia; p45: Swindon
Museum and Art Gallery, Mary Evans Picture Library/Francis Frith; p48: Ambross 07/Wikipedia; p49: Mary Evans Picture Library/
The Womens Library; p51: Roger Cracknell 01/classic/Alamy; p53: Illustrate London News Ltd/Mary Evans; p55: Terence
Mendoza/Shutterstock, York Museums Trust (Castle Museum); p58: Hazeelin Hassan/Shutterstock; p59: Thomas Owen Jenkins/
Shutterstock, Juriah Mosin/Shutterstock; p61: Maurice Savage/Alamy.

All other images copyright of Hometown World

Every effort has been made to trace and acknowledge the ownership of copyright.
If any rights have been omitted, the publishers offer to rectify this in any future editions.

Written by Jim Pipe
Educational consultant: Neil Thompson
Local history consultant: Mark Latham
Designed by Sarah Allen

Illustrated by Kate Davies, Dynamo Ltd, Peter Kent, John MacGregor,
Leighton Noyes, Nick Shewring and Tim Sutcliffe.
Additional photographs by Alex Long

First published by HOMETOWN WORLD in 2011
Hometown World Ltd
7 Northumberland Buildings
Bath BA1 2JB

www.hometownworld.co.uk

Copyright © Hometown World Ltd 2011
ISBN 978-1-84993-210-3
All rights reserved
Printed in China

CELT
500 BC

ROMAN
AD 43–410

ANGLO-SAXON
AD 450–1066

VIKING
AD 865–1066

MEDIEVAL TIMES
1066–1485